**this
strawberry
book
belongs
to:**

this book
is for
Marc
and
Timmy
and
the two
Christophers

the strawberry
word
book
by Richard Hefter

strawberry books • distributed by Larousse & Co., Inc. • New York

on the farm

tree

cow

sheep

grass

fence

ducks

hen

flowers

chick

rake

farmer

barn

silo

tractor

gate

goat

stream

bucket

goose

pig

egg

acrobat

tightrope walker

strongman

ringmaster

juggler

tiger

lion tamer

lion

on the ranch

hat

moustache

vest

chaps

lariat

dog

post

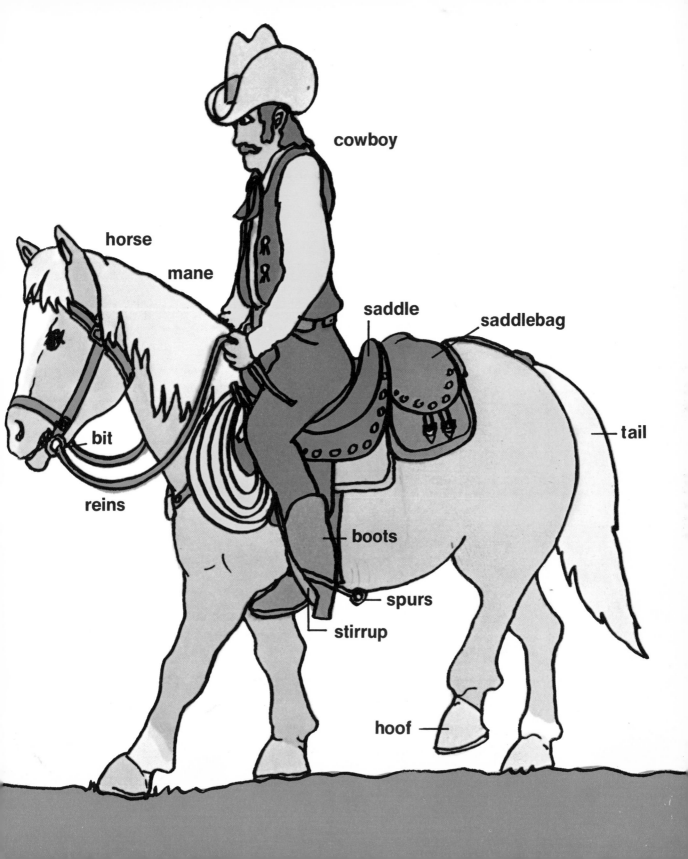

cowboy

horse

mane

saddle

saddlebag

tail

bit

reins

boots

spurs

stirrup

hoof

at the beach

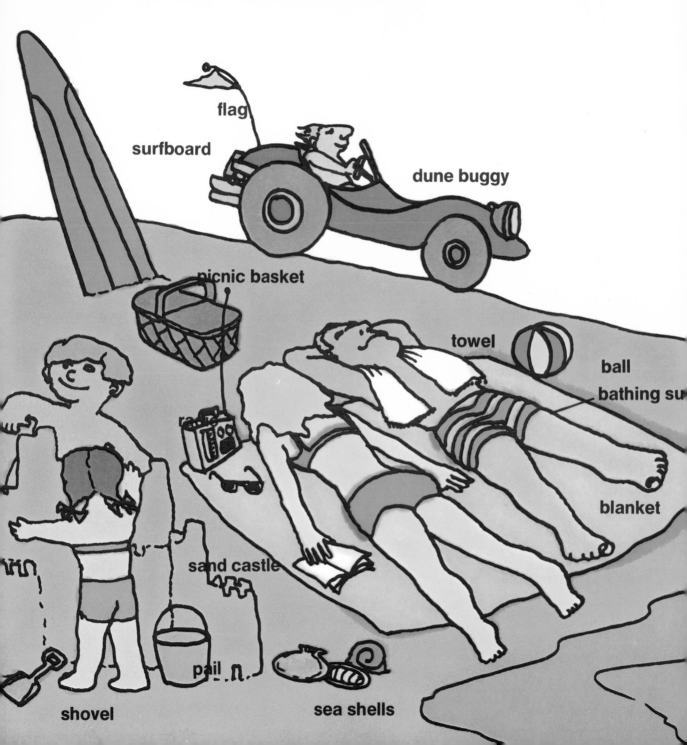

flag

surfboard

dune buggy

picnic basket

towel

ball

bathing su

blanket

sand castle

pail

shovel

sea shells

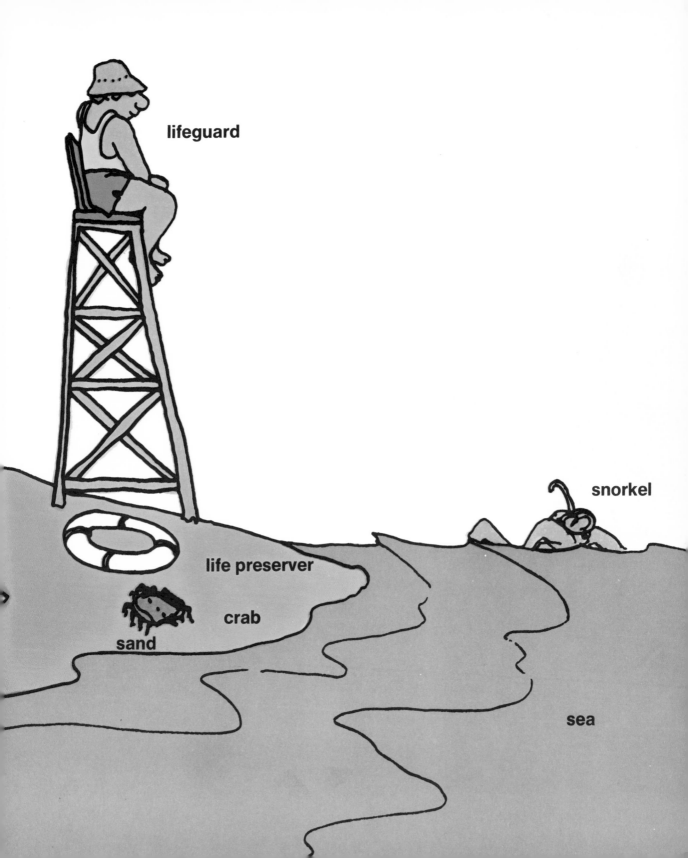

lifeguard

snorkel

life preserver

crab

sand

sea

on the street

building

bricklayer

hat

plumber

pipe

overalls

bricks

mortar

trowel

wrench

screwdriver

screws

brush

carpenter

hammer

painter

paint

plumb bob

window

lumber

bathtub

saw horse

ladder

saw

level

ruler

nails

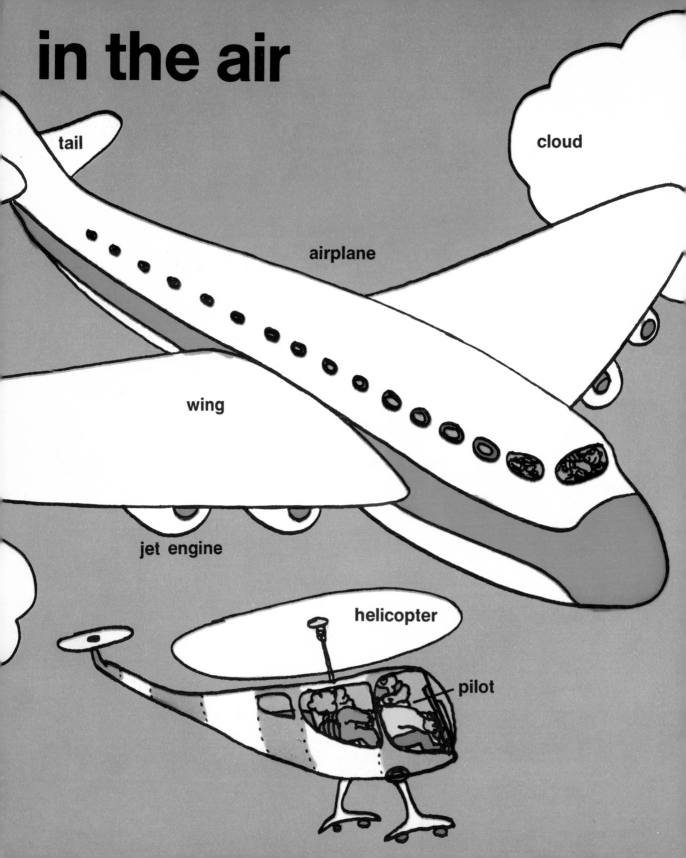

balloon

balloonist

bird

parachute

basket

control tower

airport

runway

on the water

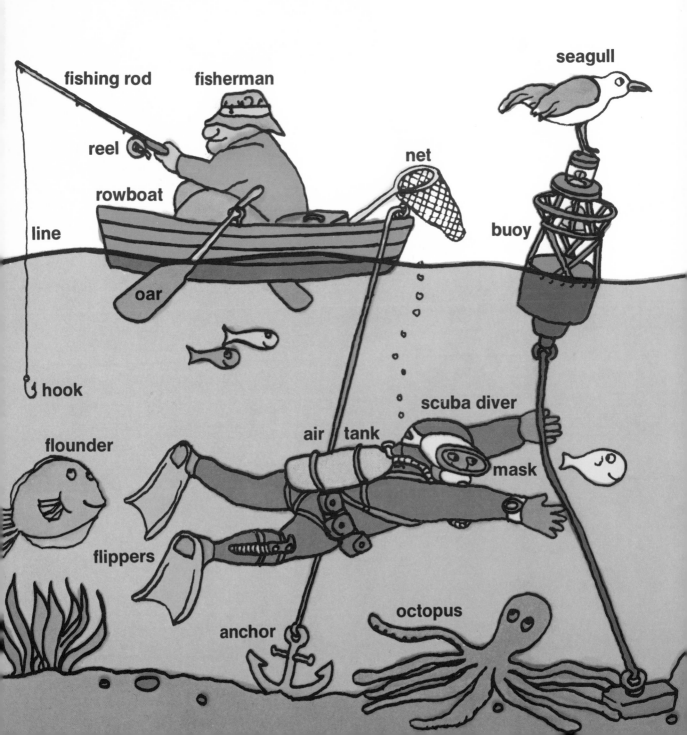

fishing rod

fisherman

reel

rowboat

line

oar

hook

flounder

flippers

net

seagull

buoy

scuba diver

air tank

mask

anchor

octopus

sail

sailor

sailboat

rudder

shark

starfish

lobster

at the station

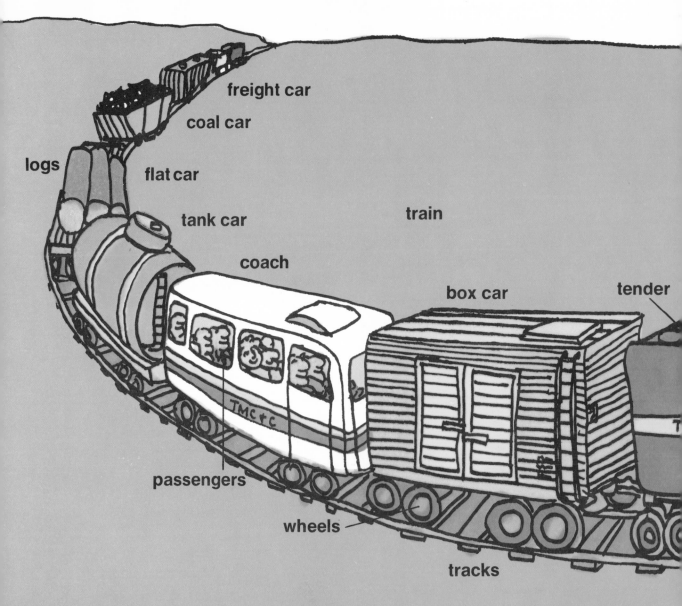

freight car

coal car

logs

flat car

tank car

train

coach

box car

tender

TMC+C

passengers

wheels

tracks

baggage

platform

on the road

hill

garage

station wagon

tow truck

STOP

stop sign

motorcycle

policeman

around the house

living room

couch

lamp

television

cushion

cat

candle

candlestick

rug

table

books

shade

telephone

armchair

book case

wall

clock

door

toilet

sink

doorknob

stairway

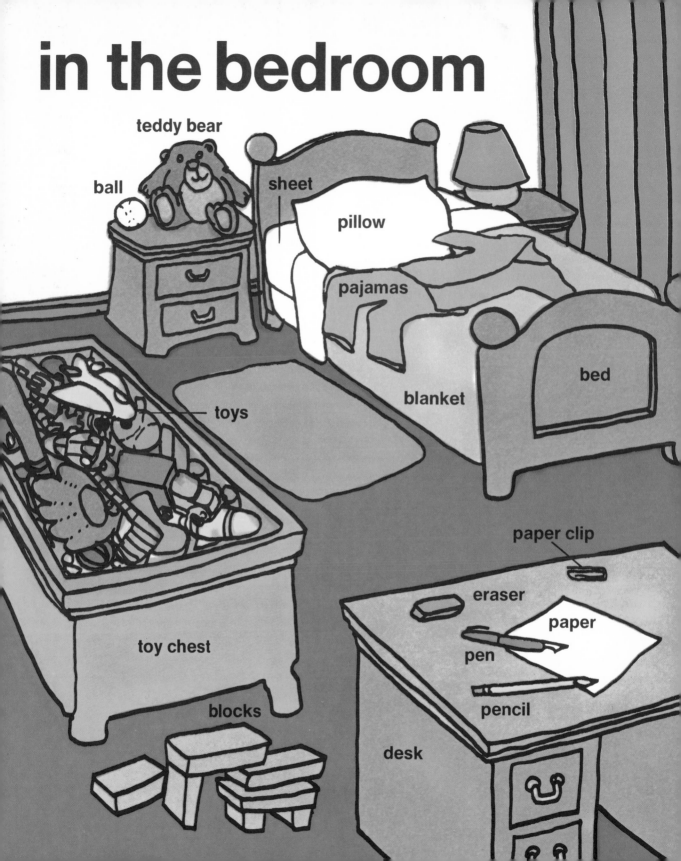

in the bedroom

teddy bear

ball

sheet

pillow

pajamas

toys

blanket

bed

paper clip

eraser

paper

pen

pencil

toy chest

blocks

desk

closet

globe

pants

shirt

shoes

drum

electric train

in the kitchen

window

refrigerator

can

lid

jar

pot

kettle

shelf

wall

box

sink

faucet

frying pan

stove

drawer

floor

at the table

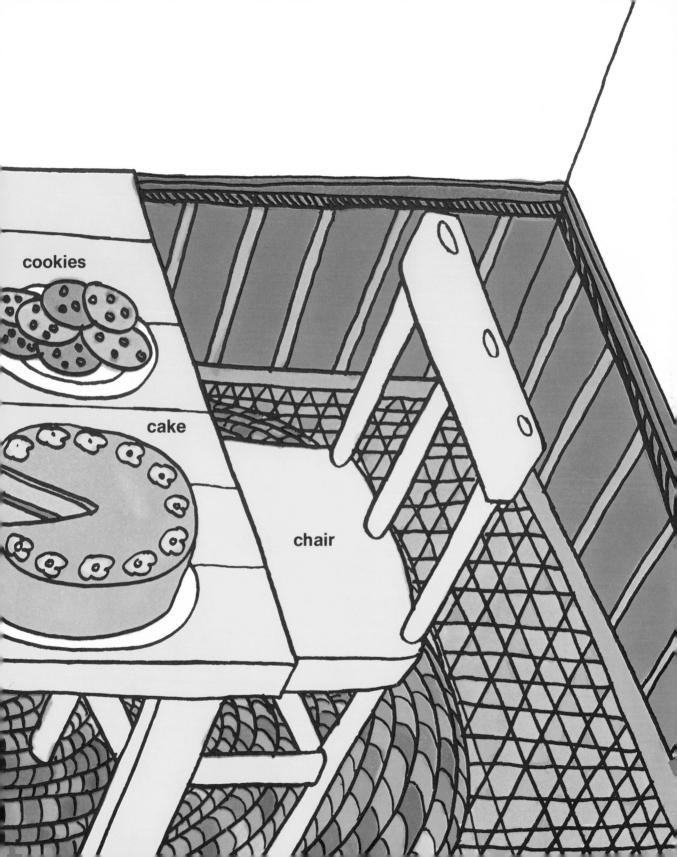

fruit

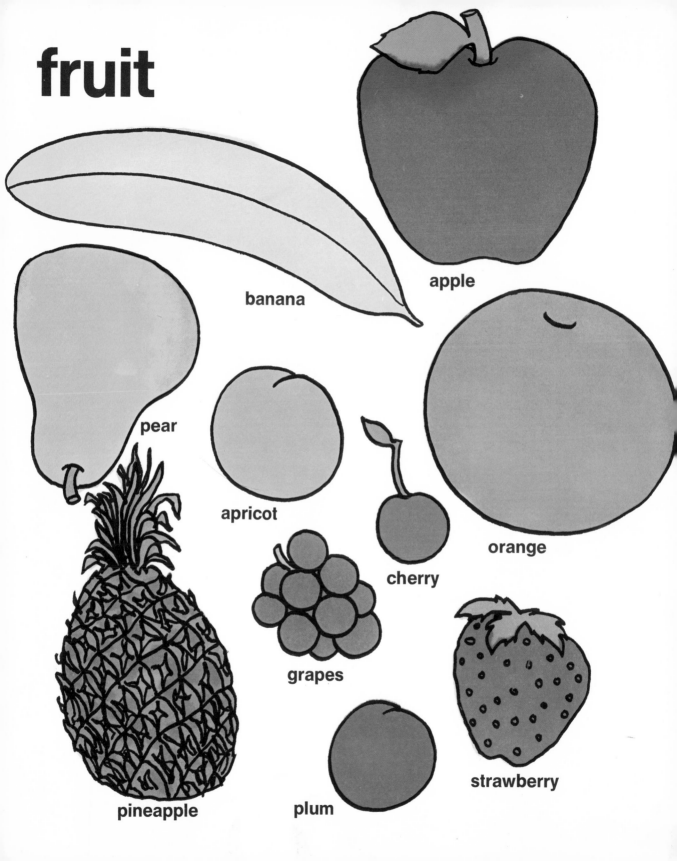

banana

apple

pear

apricot

cherry

orange

grapes

pineapple

plum

strawberry